ESSENTIALLY ENGLISH

photographs by patrick ward

For my daughter Jo, who has yet to discover her England

First published in Great Britain in 2003 by
Michael O'Mara Books Limited
9 Lion Yard, Tremadoc Road
London SW4 7NQ

A CIP catalogue record for this book is available from the British Library

ISBN 1-84317-003-5

1 3 5 7 9 10 8 6 4 2

Designed and typeset by www.glensaville.com

Colour Origination by Colourwise Ltd

Printed and bound by Tien Wah Press, Singapore

Author's Acknowledgements
I would like to thank my editor, Karen Dolan, and also Toby Buchan, for patiently restoring remnants of the English language to my captions and Introduction,
Glen Saville for flattering the photographs with his deceptively simple design, and
David Bann and the folk at Colourwise for gently persuading me to part with the slides so that they could get on with producing the book.
Finally, a special thank you to Val Mattingley, whose charm opened even the most difficult doors, and to Jean Ritch in Florida, a true Anglophile and this book's guardian angel.

Introduction

After spending much of the past three years photographing the English at leisure, I can well believe that Rhodes was right. We English, having moved on from the drudgery of the Industrial Revolution and the responsibilities of Empire, seem to have reached a happy plateau, where those of us not actually winning the lottery each week are giving a pretty good impersonation of having done so. Unlike our American cousins, who sternly stick to their Victorian work ethic, we often give the impression of working only on those days not taken up with our much more demanding social calendar.

Of course, quite a few of these social activities are direct spin-offs from our famous — some would say infamous — class system. Events such as the Henley Royal Regatta and Royal Ascot, both of which start early in the week and last for five days, could only take place in a country where there are substantial middle and upper classes, whose members have both time on their hands and money to burn. Being a believer in democracy, and of vaguely leftish leanings, I am a little embarrassed to admit that many of the English events like these that I most enjoy photographing simply couldn't occur in a more egalitarian society.

Besides, the English, of whatever background, are such lovely people to photograph. I used to think that their innate diffidence and modesty meant that they refused to believe that I was actually pointing my camera at them, but I have come to the conclusion that we are, in fact, involved in a mutual conspiracy. My subjects know exactly what I am up to, but tolerate my intrusions as long as I remain a kindly and faithful witness — an agreement I happily embrace.

Our much maligned weather also helps, as unlikely as that may sound. Like all serious photographers, I started out believing that you had to have the sun over your left shoulder to achieve the best results. I soon learned that this is not so, for in England the sun rarely glances over either shoulder, or anywhere else for that matter. But here's the curious thing . . . our dull and rainy conditions produce the most beautiful and luminous light, a light that allows one to see and record the life and character in people's faces, and all those subtle and fleeting expressions which would be lost under harsh sunlight. In addition, the English countryside looks so lush and green, thanks to all those downpours.

I started taking photographs back in the 1960s, definitely running before I could walk. It was a period that saw the launch – indeed, perhaps the golden age – of the Sunday newspaper colour supplements, and by my mid-twenties I was already travelling through Latin America and Mexico on open-ended assignments. Looking back, I can hardly believe I had the effrontery to accept commissions to record these very different cultures and to imagine that I had something relevant to say about them. My excuse has to be that I set out with an innocent eye, and that my pictures were accepted and published in a more innocent age.

Forty years on, though not, I hasten to add, much wiser, I felt ready to make a record of the England I love. Please note that these pictures are simply about the English – the Scots, the Welsh and the Northern Irish are really very different, and have, as they deserve, their own gifted photographers to do them justice. Of course, I have been exploring England for many years, but mostly on assignments, and therefore with the needs of editors and clients very much in mind. One of the rewards of shooting *Essentially English* was being able to go back to the basics of being a photographer, which for me meant setting out each day with a couple of small cameras, three lenses, and the firm intention of shooting only the photos I wanted to shoot. Photographer friends who started out with me in the 60s, and who have kept faith with the philosophy that less equipment equals more good photos, will be pleased to hear that the three lenses gradually crept down to two and, occasionally, even to one. Perhaps I should explain that, back then, we all worshipped the great French photographer Henri Cartier-Bresson, who travelled the world producing masterpieces with a single Leica camera. Among other things, this book is certainly my homage to him.

Making these pictures was almost always fun, and occasionally blissful. When you are in the right place at the right time, and as a result are able to capture a fleeting and special moment for others to enjoy later, then being a photographer seems to be a very special privilege indeed. The instants recorded in this book are not life-and-death moments. They are mainly small fragments of time, understated, even gentle, but I hope that collectively they speak affectionately of the English, and of the many ways in which they enjoy themselves. I am very aware that there is another, tougher, harsher, less placid England out there, but I am equally sure that there is another, tougher photographer busily recording it for a very different volume. This book is about an England that many people believe has disappeared, but which continues to flourish, an England in which people of all age groups and classes can be seen to be having a great deal of fun together. They are involved in so many activities that, were you to follow in my footsteps, you would need a few years to see all that I have seen and photographed.

Perhaps this is a good moment to mention that all the photos in this book are unposed, captured moments. The reality is that the things people actually get up to, especially in their leisure time, are so full of spontaneity and humour that there is no way I could compete with the variety and richness of real life, nor would I wish to. I would add, however, that I believe that photographers do carry around with them a storehouse of personal images, and that they perhaps go out into the world and use their cameras to bring back confirmation of those images. Certainly, in photographing the English, my own feelings and attitudes have inevitably coloured the images you see here.

I hope that these photos, as a collection, give some sense of what I feel being essentially English amounts to. They offer, I am aware, a very selective view of a very complex people. The England I have chosen to record is peopled largely by healthy and contented souls, playing out their games and rituals against an understated landscape that is very much on a human scale. Being English for me, and I feel for many of the people in these pictures, is about belonging to an extended family. Despite there being some 50 million of us crammed into a very small country, or perhaps because of it, we do enjoy a shared history, culture and common interests. The chances are that most of us will be discussing the same news, the same issues and the same scandals over the breakfast table each morning. Perhaps that is an over-simplification, because I know that this is also a divided society, divided by class, by opportunity and by race. The truth may be that I have simply photographed the English and the England that I know and love, a people and a country that I instinctively recognize and feel at home with — my own particular extended family.

This book may well suggest that there is a host of smaller tightly knit families in England, too, families with their own special dress codes for their own unique pastimes and ceremonies. Some of this is about class and some of it is about ritual. You only have to visit the Royal Enclosure at Ascot, with its elegant and apparently aristocratic visitors, to realize that much of English pomp and circumstance is only skin deep. The voices you hear around you are only occasionally of the expected cut-glass variety, and you very quickly realize that, beneath the formal morning dress and the fine millinery, a much wider cross-section of the English now enjoy this and other events that were previously open only to a privileged few. So if we are all becoming more democratic, why are we, like the couples dancing through the Cornish streets of Helston each spring, still dressing up like lords and ladies? Well, in a world where most of us now seem to live in jeans and T-shirts, there's a lot of fun to be had in living another life for a few hours, and even in crossing the social boundaries into another class. Sometimes, too, it's about returning to childhood. Dress up smartly to gain entrance to the Henley Royal Regatta's Steward's Enclosure, and you will find yourself surrounded by respectable old gentlemen rowers happily reliving their schooldays, dressed accordingly in their striped blazers and tiny caps.

Perhaps there is a longing in all of us to be someone else for a while, whether it's a saintly Druid on Primrose Hill, a Pearly King celebrating the Harvest Festival, or a young man in Hyde Park yearning to be a glamour girl in the annual Gay Parade. England, with its tolerance, its humour, its love for the eccentric, and its innate sense of the human comedy, is a pretty good place to let your hair down and do these things, and many others as well.

Recently my twenty-four-year-old daughter reminded me that, as yet, she has hardly seen England at all. She has taken off on many journeys, but they were not to Cornwall or the Lake District, but to Thailand and Australia. Like me at her age, she quite understandably feels that England can wait, while the big wide world really can't. This book, then, aims gently to suggest to her and all who read it that England, and the English, are too good a treat to miss, and that they really shouldn't delay. I am the first to admit that I may have seen it all through somewhat rose-tinted lenses, but if you have just a little romance in your soul, I hope you will too.

Patrick Ward

Patrick Ward, London, December 2002

Broadstairs Folk Week, Kent The genteel seaside resort of Broadstairs, with its Dickensian connections, Victorian lanes and grand Edwardian parade, provides the perfect setting for a week of folk concerts, dances and workshops.

Many of the events are free, including this display by a traditionally dressed group of Morris dancers cavorting along the Parade.

Tann Hill Sheep Show, Yorkshire Dales The annual Sheep Show, which takes place at the end of May, is named after the Tann Hill pub. Perched at the northern end of the Pennine Way, Tann Hill is a windswept and lonely place, even at that time of year.

It is not surprising that such a harsh landscape should produce shepherds just as tough and stoical as their flocks, but the bleakness is lightened by the brass band, the flowing ale and the camaraderie between farmers and shepherds.

Royal Ascot, Berkshire On each day of this celebrated race meeting, the Queen and her family parade in horse-drawn carriages to the Royal Enclosure, where suitably dressed guests await their arrival. Only then can racing commence.

These racegoers, complete with elegant Daimler limousine, have left the Royal
Enclosure to create their own private lunch party in the car park.

Entry into Ascot's Royal Enclosure is by invitation only, and for gentlemen morning dress and top hat are mandatory. Ascot has a special breed of guardians, affable but firm, who make sure that sartorial standards are maintained.

Thursday is, by tradition, Ladies' Day at Ascot, when the challenge is to bend the dress and hat rules sufficiently to get one's picture into the next day's newspapers.

Them and Us at Royal Ascot: This is the view of the Royal Enclosure from the Public Enclosure.

Racehorse Training, Middleham, North Yorkshire Early morning on the Yorkshire moors, as a string of racehorses make their way home from their training gallops. Waking at dawn in this small town to the sound of clattering hooves is a magical experience.

Birling Gap, East Sussex The white cliffs along the southern coast retain a certain symbolism as a bulwark against invasion. It is easy to imagine that this couple are not merely exercising their dog, but in fact reassuring themselves of England's coastal defences.

Pop Concert, Brighton Beach, East Sussex On a less defended shore, 250,000 fans gather to pay homage to wizard DJ Fat Boy Slim.
Beyond them, Brighton's magnificent but rotting West Pier awaits its long-promised restoration.

Autumn Equinox, London The Druids were originally an ancient order of pre-Christian priests. High on Primrose Hill,
a park offering panoramic views over London, they gather to celebrate their Harvest Festival.

Salvation Army Service, St Ives, Cornwall They may seem an anachronism, blowing their horns and singing hymns on a windswept Cornish beach, but everyone appreciates this particular army's good works.

Punch-and-Judy Show, Broadstairs, Kent Mr Punch has been entrancing children since the 1660s, contriving to murder his baby, his wife and a policeman, all in half an hour flat. Somehow this carnage still makes hilarious entertainment.

Kite Festival, Weymouth, Dorset This traditional seaside resort on the Dorset coast combines its all-too-brief summer tourist season with the perfect conditions for a kite-flying competition.

Brighton Beach, East Sussex Even on a summer's day, the surf can be both cold and rough. Behind these
brave youngsters rises Brighton's magnificent Palace Pier, first opened in 1891.

Sandcastle Competition, Bognor, West Sussex The tides allow only three hours for the annual Sandcastle Competition — just long enough for the creations to be built, judged and then gently dissolve beneath the waves.

Aldeburgh Carnival, Suffolk On the steps of Aldeburgh's fifteenth-century Moot Hall: the Town Crier, the bewigged Town Clerk, the Lady Mayoress and the newly elected Beauty Queen pass judgement on the annual Carnival Parade.

The holiday and fishing community of Aldeburgh on the Suffolk coast is also famous for its Benjamin Britten music festival. Its Carnival parade is always led by the band of the Welsh Guards.

Helston Floral Dance, Cornwall It's 7.30 am on a May morning in the small market town of Helston, and most of its residents are already on the streets, celebrating their annual 'Furry' Dance, and welcoming the coming of spring.

By midday the men of Helston have donned morning dress, and their ladies ballgowns, as they dance their way through the town, and in and out of each others' homes and shops.

Blessing the Sea, Hastings, East Sussex With the Town Crier and Aldermen in attendance, the Hastings lifeboat provides a fitting pulpit for a service to bless the sea, and to remember those of the town's fishing community who have died at sea.

Glastonbury Pilgrimage, Somerset Glastonbury is said to be the site of the earliest church in the British Isles, founded around AD 64. The Abbey provides a dramatic backdrop for pilgrimages.

Hobby Horse Festival, Padstow, Cornwall On May Day two 'Obby Osses', or wooden puppet hobby horses, cavort through this fishing village, lured on by their club-waving 'Teasers' and accompanied by accordionists and drummers.

Fertility rites lurk not too far beneath the surface, and it is said that if a Padstow girl is pinched by the man dancing beneath the Hobby Horse, she will be guaranteed a husband and baby within the year, though not necessarily in that order.

Passing-Out Parade, Sandhurst, Surrey This parade is the climax to a year of rigorous military training and weeks of spit and polish, as these young army officer cadets graduate to become subalterns, under the critical eye of their inspecting officer, the Duke of Edinburgh.

After the Passing-Out Parade, and the awarding of the Swords of Honour to the most outstanding cadets, the Duke, himself an ex-naval officer, stops to chat with a group of spritely soldiers from another generation on the steps of the Academy's Old Building.

Arsenal Homecoming, London There is no mistaking this little girl's devotion to the Arsenal Football Club. It is May 2002 and her team has just achieved the Double by winning both the League Premiership and the FA Cup.

Trafalgar Square, London Within minutes of England defeating Argentina in the World Cup in May 2002, the lions surrender to delirious fans celebrating their victory.

Trafalgar Day Parade, London Royal Naval Sea Cadets parade in Trafalgar Square, in the shadow of Admiral Lord Nelson's statue, to celebrate his defeat of the combined French and Spanish fleet in the epic battle off Cape Trafalgar in 1805.

Garden Fête, Guiting Power, Gloucestershire A brass band remains a staple ingredient of an English garden fête, but for this young man more modern distractions beckon.

Remembrance Sunday, London Three Chelsea Pensioners, all old enough to have fought in World War II, gather early in November at the Royal Artillery Memorial at Hyde Park Corner, to remember their fallen comrades.

Royal Hospital Founder's Day, Chelsea, London The home of the Chelsea Pensioners was founded by King Charles II 'for the succour and relief of veterans broken by age and war'. These particular veterans, whose average age is in the eighties, remain gloriously unbroken.

Garter Ceremony, Windsor Castle, Berkshire Once a year the Queen and her Knights of the fourteenth-century Order of the Garter attend a service in St George's Chapel.

Buckingham Palace Garden Party, London For some, letters from the Lord Chamberlain's Office contain invitations to one of the Queen's three midsummer garden parties. This is the Sovereign's way of thanking her subjects for their contribution to society.

Pearlies' Harvest Festival, St Martin-in-the-Fields, London The Pearly Kings and Queens, London costermongers originally elected
by street traders to protect them from interlopers and bullies, are now better known for their charity work.

Lord Mayor's Show, London The City of London's first Lord Mayor was appointed by King John in the thirteenth century. This stern judge, and his dummy *alter ego*, are awaiting the start of the Lord Mayor's procession, held each November.

Combined Cavalry Parade, Hyde Park, London Each spring retired officers from prestigious cavalry regiments congregate
in the Park to pay homage to their fallen comrades, and to reminisce over battles won and lost.

This parade could also be seen as a tribute to Savile Row, London's home of fine tailoring, for nowhere else could such perfectly cut suits, tilted bowlers or tightly furled brollies be seen.

Threlkeld Shepherds' Show, Lake District Mr J Birkett of Coniston judging the Shepherd's Crooks and Walking Sticks.
They range from Best Horn-headed Crook, through Best Wood-headed Walking Stick, to Best Lady's Stick.

For all the competitors this must be a true labour of love, since the top prize —
for Best Stick in Show — is a modest £5.

Victorian Weekend, Kirkby Lonsdale, Cumbria Life in Victorian England must have been short and brutal for many working folk, but nostalgia provides a kindly filter during this celebration of a Victorian Weekend, where only the good times are remembered.

Brass bands, period costumes, double swings and other simple pastimes perhaps remind us that the Victorian life of shared hardships was also a life of shared pleasures and companionship.

Yorkshire Grouse Moor As the mist clears on the moors, this experienced Gun, with his pair of shotguns and his gun dog at the ready, waits behind a butt for the beaters to drive the grouse into his line of fire.

Pheasant Shoot, North of England Here, in between drives, beaters sit chatting on their trailer, which is also doubling as the game cart.

Blencathra Hunt, Lake District The Blencathra Hunt – a foot pack – continues to meet on the barren hills above Keswick. Up here in the biting cold, life's issues seem more certain. The fox is definitely the enemy, and the farmer's stock needs protecting.

If you have the stamina to spend the day following the Blencathra's wily old Master of Hounds across these desolate moors, the chances are that you'll agree that he's doing a job that needs to be done.

Malham Show, Yorkshire Dales Hand-built dry-stone walls are a defining feature of the Yorkshire Dales. Beyond this one, a group of young riders awaits its turn to compete in the Show's equestrian events.

The Yorkshire Dales breed a special kind of hero who is capable of running across hills and mountains at miraculous speeds, defying all the laws of gravity as he does so. This young man, competing in the Malham Show's cross-country event, has the steely look of such a hero.

Gay Parade, Hyde Park, London He is a brave soul with strong convictions, because first he had to cross the green expanse of Hyde Park on those high heels, before he could let his hair down and become 'her' for the start of the annual Gay Parade.

As, with whistles blowing, the Parade marches forth from Hyde Park on to the bemused streets of Central London, a group of pink-clad dancers provides a joyous send-off.

Chelsea Flower Show, London It seems fitting that this most prestigious of flower shows should be recorded for posterity by a Chelsea Pensioner, for the show takes place each spring in the grounds of his residence, the Royal Hospital.

On the Show's final day a bell is rung at 5pm, and a great sell-off of the flowers and plants commences. For the next few hours the streets surrounding the showground overflow with gardening fanatics staggering home beneath their floral trophies.

Queen's Birthday Parade ('Trooping the Colour'), Horse Guards Parade, London The Queen's official birthday is always celebrated on the second Saturday in June when she, as Colonel-in-Chief of the regiments of Foot Guards, inspects their 'Colours'.

The Colours are precious historical objects and once used to be carried into battle. They are the embodiments of a regiment's ancestry and pride, to be protected at any cost to life or limb. It is these Colours that the Queen has come to inspect.

Wedding Reception, Henley-on-Thames, Oxfordshire The *Arethusa* is one of the elegant launches used by the umpires who follow competing rowers during the Henley Regatta. Here, she serves a more romantic purpose for this newlywed couple.

Golden Jubilee Party, Taggs Island, Middlesex The small and enterprising community of Taggs Island on the River Thames near Hampton Court produced a life-size cut-out of the Queen and her Consort to attend their Golden Jubilee party.

Eton Wall Game, Eton College, Berkshire In November, two teams of Eton schoolboys meet in the annual Wall Game. This rugger-style scrum is called a 'bully', and the teams are struggling to reach the goals at each end of the wall.

London Marathon This is one of the world's great Marathons, both for the vast numbers of competitors it attracts, and for the splendid route it traces for twenty-six-and-a-bit miles.

Swan Upping, River Thames The Vintners and Dyers, two of London's ancient livery companies, have the right to keep swans on the Thames between London Bridge and Henley. Each summer they make a five-day voyage upriver to confirm these privileges.

This they do by capturing the swans and their cygnets, and then marking the cygnets' beaks, with one nick for the Dyers and two for the Vintners. Their skill ensures that the swans suffer nothing more than a brief loss of dignity.

Great River Race, Richmond, Surrey With 300 rowing boats of every shape and size, carrying some 2,000-odd competitors, this race between Richmond and Greenwich has become the Marathon of the River Thames, and attracts its fair share of colourful characters.

Thames fishermen, Hampton, Middlesex Fishing is England's most popular sporting activity — among men, at least. After hours of rain, these anglers were eventually rewarded by the sun breaking through, and the arrival of their partners with refreshments.

Thames Traditional Boat Rally, Henley-on-Thames, Oxfordshire For the past few years Lyndon Yorke, a true English eccentric, has graced the Traditional Boat Rally, most recently with his two-seater steam-powered *Dreadnought*.

The Rally encourages owners of traditional craft to restore and cherish them for posterity, and attracts some 300 entries, including slipper launches, gentlemen's day launches, steam canoes, and these much-loved and much-varnished rowing boats.

Shiplake Regatta, River Thames, Oxfordshire A few miles upriver from Henley's Royal Regatta, Shiplake celebrates a rather more relaxed event with the evening greasy-pole competition.

Fourth of June, Eton College, Berkshire Eton celebrates the birthday of King George III with a procession of skiffs on the River Thames. Boys dressed in nineteenth-century naval uniforms stand to salute Eton, Queen and Country.

Battle of Hastings, Battle, East Sussex In perhaps the most decisive battle in English history the forces of William, Duke of Normandy, defeated those of King Harold II in 1066. In this re-enactment, William the Conqueror will once again triumph.

Battle of Stamford Hill, Bude, Cornwall Englishmen relive another battle, this one from 1643, when Sir Ralph Hopton and Sir Bevill Grenville led their 3,000 Cornish troops to victory against superior Roundhead forces.

Medieval Fair, Battle, East Sussex Trading heavily on its associations with the Battle of Hastings in 1066, the market town of Battle holds its Medieval Fair each May, complete with bed of nails and bloodthirsty audience.

Aldeburgh Carnival, Suffolk Ye Olde Marine Regatta and Carnival began in the nineteenth century, and has remained relatively unchanged for the past fifty years.

Weymouth Carnival, Dorset The annual carnival procession in this Dorset seaside resort has too many mechanized floats, but is saved by its lively and humorous townsfolk, including these flowering participants.

Not an audience Weymouth would wish to disappoint! These ladies had claimed a commanding viewpoint outside their beachfront hotel from which to judge the carnival.

Birdman Competition, Bognor Regis, West Sussex Later in the day, men and women will attempt to fly off the end of Bognor's pier, but first a band plays its heart out along the seafront to let visitors know of the madness to come.

Some contestants come to amuse the vast crowd lining the beach; others are the serious chaps with their complex and aerodynamic flying machines, who strive to fly off the pier, and cover the 100 metres that will win them a £25,000 prize. They are still trying!

Henley Royal Regatta, Henley-on-Thames, Oxfordshire The grandest event in the English rowing season, only the two world wars have interrupted this Regatta, which otherwise has taken place every year since 1839.

Though perfectly attired for the exclusive Stewards' Enclosure, this couple chose to view the races from the river bank, while the umpires made their stately progress in launches behind each race.

Malham, Yorkshire Dales The countryside around the village of Malham, with its dry-stone walls and single-track lanes, is quintessential Yorkshire Dales. It is also sheep-raising country and, as this motorist found out, sheep *do* have right of way.

Near Malham Cove, Yorkshire Dales A footpath follows a stream from the village of Malham to the Cove, where skilled rock climbers challenge its sheer and forbidding rockface. These young adventurers, taking more tentative steps, were encountered en route to the cove.

Malham Show, Yorkshire Dales This small country show is one Yorkshire's most enjoyable events. Despite the rain, there are sheep to be presented, heavy horses to be decorated, stone walls to be built, and fell races to be run.

Everyone at this Show seems wholly involved, with even the prizewinning cattle seeming to share in the happy atmosphere.

Malham Show, Yorkshire Dales The show ends on a noisy note, with a motorcycle scramble. For these kids the temptation to get spattered with flying mud as the bikes hurtled off the start line proved too much. As it did for this photographer, too.

Three Peaks Cycle Race, Yorkshire Dales This twenty-two-mile marathon across Yorkshire's three highest peaks is billed as a cycle race, but much of the course is so tortuous that the machines have to be either pushed or carried on their riders' backs.

Bolton Priory, Yorkshire Dales Beneath the ruins of the Priory of St Mary and St Cuthbert runs the River Wharfe. A group of Augustinian priests first occupied this site in 1154, and signs of their presence are still visible in the Priory's ruined High Altar.

Above Malham Cove, Yorkshire Dales The perfect classroom . . . the area around the village of Malham is known as a school for geologists, and this student, assisted by his mother, is exploring the mysteries of the strange limestone pavements above the Cove.

Tolpuddle Martyrs' Parade, Tolpuddle, Dorset In 1834 six Dorset farm labourers were transported to an Australian penal colony for forming a trade union. The ensuing public outcry led to their being returned home after serving less than half of their seven-year sentences.

Each summer a happy gathering of members of the trade-union movement parade their colourful banners through the picture-postcard village, to celebrate the more enlightened society for which they, and their forebears, have fought.

Bugatti Owners' Club Rally, Prescott Hill, Gloucestershire On a Sunday in July, the faithful gather in the Cotswolds to worship an automotive masterpiece designed by an Italian engineer in the 1920s, and built in France. This legendary vehicle is the Bugatti.

After picnicking beside their cars, owners proudly parade them up Prescott Hill. No racing here, for the track is too narrow and the Bugattis far too precious to risk damaging — just a gentlemanly run against the clock.

Rolls-Royce Meeting, West Dean Gardens, Chichester, West Sussex Billed as 'Hampers and Champers', this was a gathering of traditional Rolls-Royces, plus the occasional Bentley, and their devoted keepers.

The arrival of a Rolls-Royce hearse at the Meeting might suggest even more the passing of an automotive era, but the undertaker owner had put her to an altogether jollier use — providing the champagne, wines and spirits for the occasion.

Scuttlebrook Wake, Chipping Campden, Gloucestershire The Wake derives its name from the stream running beneath the site on the edge of town. Its street procession and Morris dancing have been annual summer events since the seventeenth century.

After the Grand Street Parade, led by the Bretforton Silver Band, and the crowning of the Beauty Queen, there is the maypole and Morris dancing and, for these three young fairies, the fancy-dress parade.

Ballet dancers, Hurlingham Club, London The Hurlingham Club is best known as a venue for professional tennis and vicious croquet matches, but when the Church of England held its garden party at the Club these anxious young ballet students were asked to perform.

Tango al fresco, Regent's Park, London On three Sundays each summer, Kele Baker sets up her cassette player on the Broad Walk in Regent's Park, and scores of dancers are transformed into passionate Latins as she teaches them to tango.

Cotswold Pony Sales, Gloucestershire This great sale takes place each June and October near Cirencester, and all sorts of horsey tackle are on offer as well as the ponies. Not for sale, however, is this much-cosseted English bulldog.

Dog Show, Ampney Crucis, Gloucestershire At the annual garden fête, a downpour just before the dog show meant that this woman's best friend, perfectly groomed for the event, simply had to be protected from the elements, while she and her other dog were drenched.

Derby Day, Epsom, Surrey Eccentric Mr Mario may not even be English at all but he has been adding colour to major racing events for many years and is certainly an honorary Englishman.

These open-top buses are brought out of retirement each year to provide a perfect
grandstand view of the thoroughbreds running the final furlong.

Appleby Horse Fair, Cumbria The fair has taken place each June on Fair Hill since the 1750s, and travellers still lead their horses down to the River Eden each day to wash them down beneath the town bridge, under the critical gaze of horse traders, townsfolk and tourists.

The travellers often bring their 'road racers' to Appleby — animals bred from trotting horses crossed with coloured breeds. This one is pulling a sulky, a light single-seater designed more for speed than for comfort.

DIV J
CLASS 4

DIV J
CLASS 5

Village Fête, Ellens Green, Surrey Preparations are under way for this year's village fête, and these two ladies are hard at work, tasting and passing judgement on the jams, breads and cakes entered in competition. Sadly, offers to assist in this onerous task were rejected.

Dogs, too, will be judged later in the day, and this competitor, perhaps wistfully eyeing the ice-cream van, is determined to keep her poodles cool and relaxed in the meantime.

Henley Festival of Music and the Arts, Henley-on-Thames, Oxfordshire This alfresco music festival, with its great floating stage, takes place on the site of the Henley Regatta, taking advantage of the giant stands and marquees erected for that earlier event.

Attending a music festival staged on the River Thames means that you may choose to arrive by boat. You won't be able actually to see the singers and musicians from your craft, but you will still hear them for free.

Henley Festival of Music and the Arts, Henley-on-Thames, Oxfordshire Beneath the setting sun, couples enter 'Sonic Skirts' to listen to 'three ladies in gossipy conversations', all part of an art installation created by local artist Lucie Ryan.

Glyndebourne Opera Festival, East Sussex Each afternoon from mid-May to the end of August, 800 opera lovers congregate on the immaculate lawns of Glyndebourne, a Tudor mansion on the Sussex Downs, and stake out their picnic spots before heading off to the adjoining opera house.

1940s Night, Chartwell, near Westerham, Kent These couples, dancing down memory lane to the music of the New Glenn Miller Band, are in the garden of Chartwell, a very special house. Now owned by the National Trust, it was bought by Winston Churchill in 1924.

It is interesting to ponder quite what Sir Winston would have made of this 1940s Night, with revellers dressed in the military uniforms of the British, American and even German forces, all dancing the night away on his lawn.

Fête Champêtre, Stourton, Wiltshire Dressed up for an evening of music, dancing and picnicking, these guests are making their way through the village to the Palladian Stourhead House.

Later in the evening Stourhead provides the most romantic of settings, as guests picnic by candlelight
in the landscaped gardens to the strains of a classical concert wafting across the lake.

Grasmere Sports, Lake District Hound-trailing has been enjoyed in the Lake District for more than 200 years.
The dogs eagerly pursue a pre-laid scent of aniseed and paraffin across the surrounding fields and fells.

Competitors in the Junior Fell Race, heading for the mountains, soon leave the showground far below. A few weeks later, a nearby farm plays host to the Langdale Show, with its traditional Cumberland Wrestling.

Woolsack Races, Tetbury, Gloucestershire The town celebrates its ancient connection with the wool trade by staging its annual races. The woolsacks each weigh a hefty sixty pounds, so sprinting with one is no mean feat.

Cheese Rolling, Cooper's Hill, Gloucestershire If climbing up the one-in-three incline of Cooper's Hill is a five-minute ordeal, tumbling down again in pursuit of a large and lethally accelerating Double Gloucester cheese is a thirty-second nightmare.

Heavy Horses, New Forest Show, Ringwood, Hampshire Chrystel Mouland's day started at 6.30 am, with the feeding of her two Clydesdale heavy horses, Prince and Jedburgh. It is now mid-afternoon, and all the grooming and polishing are finally bearing fruit.

All this effort is so that she and her husband Dave, and of course Prince and Jedburgh, can take part in the Ringwood Brewery Heavy Horse Musical Drive, an event of stunning precision and colour.

Clipping the Church, Painswick, Gloucestershire On a blustery autumn afternoon at St Mary's Church, the choristers and buglers bravely perform while the village children encircle the church and, holding hands, rush forward and kick the building three times.

Following the ceremony, which is said to symbolize the parishioners' affection for their church, the vicar preaches a sermon —
on this occasion while fighting, with good humour, a losing battle against the devilish wind.

May Day Parade, Moulton, Northamptonshire This is a final rehearsal for these youngsters, before they attend the crowning of their village May Queen.

Easier to smile when you are busy. . . These Morris dancers take flight as they celebrate the crowning of Moulton's chilled and less amused May Queen.

May Day Parade, Moulton, Northamptonshire Morrismen musicians lead the Parade from the park and on to each of the village's pubs, where they will stop to entertain, dance and quench their thirsts.

A pensive and beflowered Morrisman watches another troupe of dancers, while waiting to perform before the May Queen.

Veteran Car Rally, Hyde Park, London In England, up until 1908, a car had to be preceded by a man carrying a red flag, to give pedestrians fair warning. This Rally, which sets off from Hyde Park for Brighton, celebrates the repeal of this law.

Some 400 veteran cars, many of them up to 100 years old, make their leisurely way down to the coast. This is certainly not a race, for simply to complete the sixty-mile journey in these elderly machines is achievement enough.

Costermongers' Parade, Guildhall, London Mayors from London boroughs parade through the City of London
en route to the Costermongers' Service at the church of St Mary-le-Bow, Cheapside.

In the courtyard of London's Guildhall, mayors and mayoresses watching dancers before the Costermongers' Parade are joined by one of the Pearly Kings and Queens – London costermongers whose dress clothes display an extravagance of pearl buttons.

Lord Mayor's Show, London Watermen wearing their scarlet Doggett's Coat and Badge regalia prepare to join the Procession. In 1715 Thomas Doggett, an actor and comedian, created the annual rowing race for watermen which still bears his name.

These ward beadles are livery company officers whose duties include marshalling
the liverymen at the election of the Lord Mayor of London.

Royal Birthday Salute, Hyde Park, London In 1460 King James II of Scotland was killed when he stood too close to a cannon being fired in his honour. Understandable, then, that royalty now stays home when the King's Troop, Royal Horse Artillery, fires its Birthday salutes.

History in Action, Kirby Hall, Oundle, Northamptonshire The eighteenth-century Battle of New Kirby Farm, New England, is here refought in the grounds of an English country house. Fortunately, the English redcoats are only firing blanks.

History in Action, Kirby Hall, Oundle, Northamtonshire During this re-enactment of a skirmish in the Peninsular War, 1813, the Duke of Wellington's redcoats are defeated by Napoleon's army, an outcome not popular with the partisan English audience.

Time travel in an English cornfield? Not exactly — simply a French Napoleonic trooper from 1813 contemplating an American M4 Sherman tank and its crew, from 1944, preparing for the Battle for Normandy. To complicate matters further, they are all Englishmen!

Notting Hill Carnival, London Each August Bank Holiday, over a million people of every creed and colour pour on to the streets of West London to celebrate this Caribbean carnival, often described as Europe's biggest street party.

Many feel that Carnival has outgrown the increasingly gentrified streets of Notting Hill, and each year threatens to be its last in this venue. However, if you can stand the crowds and the decibels, catch it now, where it all began.

Last Night of the Proms, Hyde Park, London In 2000 there was a joyous atmosphere in Hyde Park as revellers, having enjoyed their own alfresco concert, joined in the Albert Hall's grand finale thanks to giant television screens in the Park.

A year later, in September 2001, a very different atmosphere prevailed within the Albert Hall. Four days earlier, terrorists had struck in New York, and the Promenaders showed their sympathy for the victims by waving the Stars and Stripes alongside the Union flag.

Great Dorset Steam Fair, Tarrant Hinton, Dorset This is probably the largest steam event in England, with classes for every shape and size of steam vehicle, including these miniature steam tractors attended by their doting owners.

Great Bucks Steam Working, Shabington, Buckinghamshire Engines in Steam, Invitation Steering, Musical Chairs with Steam Engines and a church service in front of Mr A E Reed's Fair Organ are all on the menu for this weekend event.

Great Dorset Steam Fair, Tarrant Hinton, Dorset Attending the thirty-third Great Working of Steam Engines, and surrounded by the haunting music of fairground organs, this gentleman seems to be lost in nostalgia, oblivious to the rain, and perhaps unaware of his headgear.

Town Criers' Competition, Hastings, East Sussex England has had town criers since the twelfth century. Ringing their bells and proclaiming 'Oyez! Oyez! Oyez!' they would bring news to their communities of coming events, disasters and births and deaths.

Regent Street Festival, London For 364 days of the year pedestrians take their lives in their hands when crossing traffic-clogged Regent Street. However, on one glorious Sunday every September, the whole of this elegantly curving Georgian avenue is closed to traffic.

Bouncy castles, carousels, scary rides, and young marching bands all take advantage of the traffic-free street, but perhaps the greatest pleasure is to be had in simply dawdling, and safely gazing up at the splendid architecture.

Wasdale Show, Lake District Beyond the starkly beautiful Wasdale Water, at Wasdale Head, the Wasdale Shepherds' Meet and Show takes place each October. With the tourist season over, this is very much a show for locals — a gathering of friends.

All the usual Lakeland pursuits take place here — the daunting fell races that see runners disappear up a cloud-ringed mountain, the Cumberland wrestling, and the judging of the white-faced Herdwick sheep.

Cambridge University May Eights Week These undergraduates, dressed as surgeons, are competing on the River Cam. The river is in places too narrow and winding for boats to race side-by-side, so teams attempt to bump the boat ahead of them.

Serious enthusiasts of all ages follow the week's racing, some hurtling along the towpath on their bicycles, while winning crews are easily recognized by the victors' garlands they wear in their hair.

Graduation Day, Cambridge University A bird's eye view, seen from the church tower of Great Saint Mary's, of undergraduates waiting to enter the Senate House to receive their degrees. The colours of the hoods indicate their degree subjects or their seniority.

A candle-lit graduation supper in the Hall of Magdalene College, with one dashing bow tie on show at this most formal occasion, and with College benefactors gazing down sternly from their portraits above the diners.

Clare College May Ball, Cambridge University The May Ball provides a fitting climax to at least three years spent as a Cambridge undergraduate. Arriving by punt not only creates a romantic entry, but also makes it difficult for gatecrashers to infiltrate the Ball.

By Cambridge standards, Clare College is neither large nor wealthy, but its Ball has a special charm, and its organizers are bright, too. They time their fireworks display so that it coincides with the much grander show put on by St John's College next door.

Clare College May Ball, Cambridge University With King's College Chapel beyond, the quadrangle of Clare College becomes a tented and glowing fantasy – the perfect setting for a night of dining and dancing, and a romantic farewell to university life.

It's five o'clock in the morning, and as a misty dawn breaks over Cambridge, couples depart in punts, heading upstream to enjoy a traditional English breakfast in the nearby village of Grantchester.